Little
Pebble™

Our Pets
Guinea Pigs

by Lisa J. Amstutz

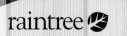
raintree

a Capstone company — publishers for children

Edited by Marissa Kirkman
Designed by Juliette Peters (cover) and Charmaine Whitman (interior)
Picture research by Morgan Walters
Production by Laura Manthe
Originated by Capstone Global Library Limited
Printed and bound in India

ISBN 978 1 4747 5712 6
21 20 19 18 17
10 9 8 7 6 5 4 3 2 1

British Library Cataloguing in Publication Data
A full catalogue record for this book is available from the British Library.

Acknowledgements
We would like to thank the following for permission to reproduce photographs: Alamy: Juniors Bildarchiv GmbH, 19; Getty Images: Steve Teague, 21; Minden Pictures: Jane Burton, 17; Shutterstock: cynoclub, top 13, Dev_Maryna, 1, 5, 9, 20, Dora Zett, back cover, Heder Zambrano, 7, Kristo-Gothard Hunor, top 11, top 15, Miroslav Hlavko, Cover, Mr Aesthetics, (wood) design element throughout, PHOTO FUN, bottom 15, Rosa Jay, 16, Suzan, bottom 13, Vera Zinkova, bottom 11

Every effort has been made to contact copyright holders of material reproduced in this book. Any omissions will be rectified in subsequent printings if notice is given to the publisher.

All the Internet addresses (URLs) given in this book were valid at the time of going to press. However, due to the dynamic nature of the Internet, some addresses may have changed, or sites may have changed or ceased to exist since publication. While the author and publisher regret any inconvenience this may cause readers, no responsibility for any such changes can be accepted by either the author or the publisher.

Contents

Listen!

Wheek!

This guinea pig is happy.

It wants a treat.

These pets make
many sounds.
They purr. They chut.
They coo.

Furry pets

Is this pet really a pig?

No! It is a rodent.

It is also called a cavy.

Some people call it a piggy.

Guinea pig fur can be
short or long.
It can have swirls.
The fur can be many colours.

Munch!

A guinea pig eats pellets.

It chews hay.

A guinea pig has 20 teeth.

It chews a lot.

This keeps its teeth short.

Growing up

Look!

New pups are born.

Can you count them?

Pups play.

They run and jump into the air.

This is called popcorning.

Play time

Guinea pigs play hide
and seek.

They run through tubes. **Peek!**

They are fun pets.

Glossary

chut short muttering sound; guinea pigs often chut when they are relaxed

coo soft sound; adult guinea pigs may coo when they "talk" to each other

hay dried field grasses

pellet small, hard piece of food

pup young guinea pig

purr low constant sound; guinea pigs may purr when they are happy and when being petted

rodent mammal with long front teeth used for gnawing

swirl chunk of hair that is twisted into a circle

wheek long, loud squeak; guinea pigs often wheek when they are excited

Read more

Gordon's Guide to Caring for Your Guinea Pig (Pets' Guides), Isabel Thomas (Raintree, 2014)

Guinea Pig: Everything You Need To Know To Look After Your Best Pal! (Pet Pals), Pat Jacobs (Wayland, 2017)

How to Look After Your Guinea Pig: A Practical Guide to Caring For Your Pet, In Step-By-Step Photographs, David Alderton (Armadillo Books, 2016)

Websites

www.bbc.co.uk/cbeebies/topics/pets
Discover a variety of pets, play pet games and watch pet videos on this fun BBC website.

www.bluecross.org.uk
Find out more about how to choose a pet and care for your pet on the Blue Cross website.

Comprehension questions

1. Name one way that guinea pigs can look different from each other.

2. Why do guinea pigs need to chew?

3. Would you like to own a guinea pig? Why or why not?

Index